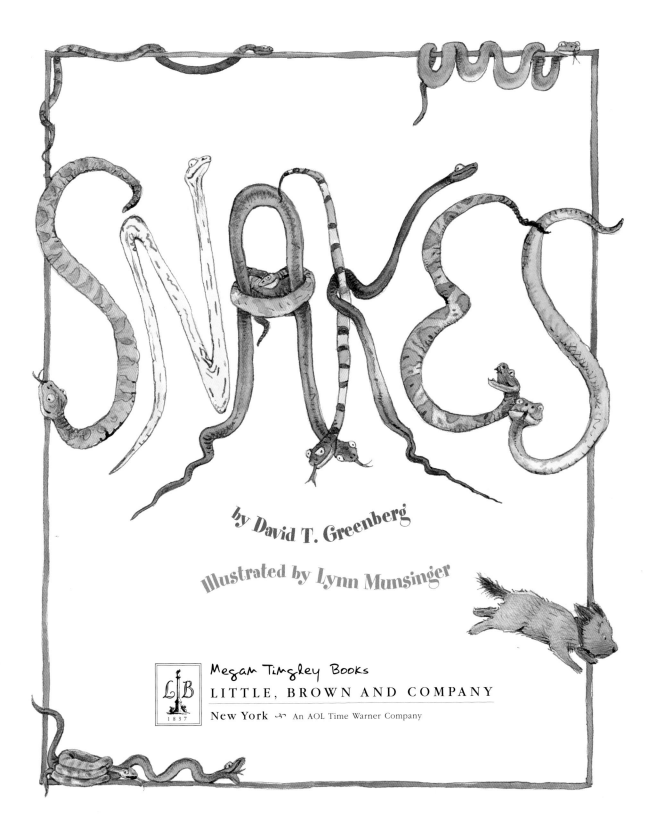

SNAKES

by David T. Greenberg

Illustrated by Lynn Munsinger

Megan Tingley Books

LITTLE, BROWN AND COMPANY

New York · An AOL Time Warner Company

To Koryna: For goodness' snake, you're twice
as beautiful as a polar bear!
—Your loving Uncle David

For Linda
—L.M.

First Edition

Library of Congress Cataloging-in-Publication Data

Greenberg, David (David T.)
Snakes! / by David T. Greenberg ; illustrated by Lynn Munsinger.
p. cm.
Summary: Suggests many unpleasant things that can be done with and to snakes, as
well as some very unpleasant things they might do to even the bravest child when they
slither from beneath the bed and fill the house.
ISBN 0-316-32076-5 (hc)
[1. Snakes—Fiction. 2. Stories in rhyme.] I. Munsinger, Lynn, ill. II. Title.
PZ8.3.G755 Sn 2003
[E]—dc21

2002075226

10 9 8 7 6 5 4 3 2 1

TWP

Printed in Singapore

The illustrations for this book were done in pen and ink and watercolor on
Waterford Saunders paper. The text was set in Catull, and the display type is Spumoni.

You're the kind of kid
Who likes to wrestle squid
Or battle in the bathtub with a shark

In no uncertain terms
You love the squirms of worms
Or hunting after werewolves in the dark

From everything we hear
You haven't any fear
(Well, hardly any fear, for goodness sakes)

There's only one exception
Now don't attempt deception
Let there be no misconception…

SNAKES!

Tangled like spaghetti
Slithery and sweaty
Nesting in a heap beneath your bed

Can you feel your mattress shaking?
Slowly they're awaking
And it's months and months and months since they have fed

With a horrifying rustle
Of cartilage and muscle
Very very slowly they unwind

Tongues abruptly flickering
Whispering and snickering
They wriggle off to see what they can find

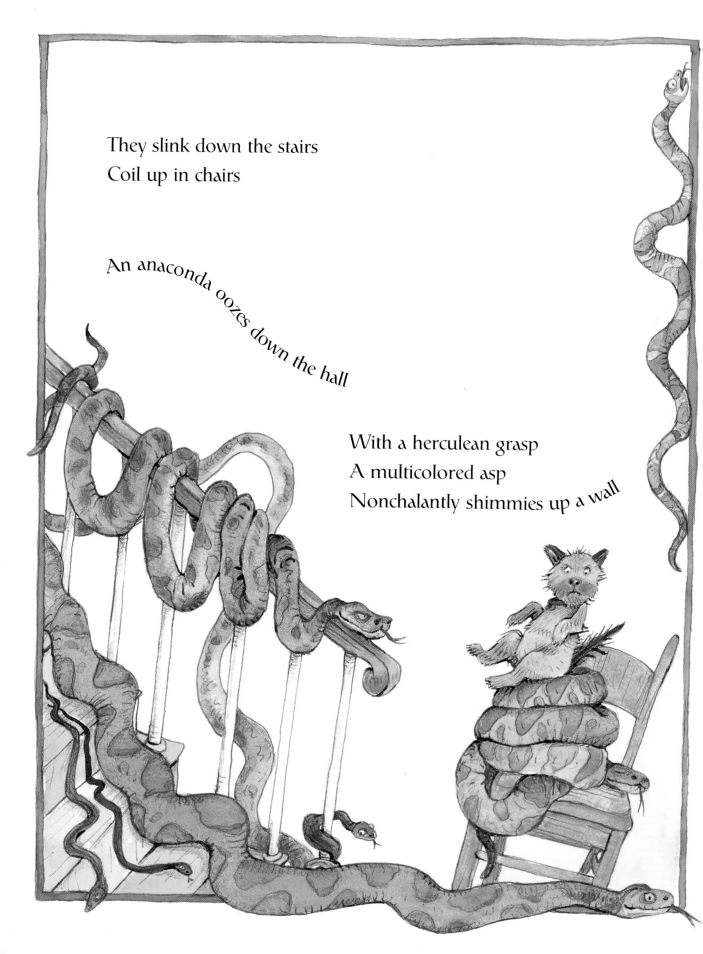

They slink down the stairs
Coil up in chairs

An anaconda oozes down the hall

With a herculean grasp
A multicolored asp
Nonchalantly shimmies up a wall

Did something brush your hair?
Perhaps a waft of air

Or is something breathing softly through its nose?

You can feel it in your ear
Hideously near

Then something heavy slides across your toes

With dread you lift your head
And circling your bed
Is a sight to give a superhero shakes

Swaying oh so gently
Watching you intently
A hundred thousand salivating snakes!

Reticulated belly snakes
Sea snakes, tree snakes
Peanut-butter jelly snakes
Hyperactive flea snakes

Antagonistic rattlesnakes
Wary snakes, hairy snakes
Dragonistic battlesnakes
Very very scary snakes

The snakes begin to roam
Through the chambers of your home
Like pyroclastic streams of melted crayon

Searching every nook
Cabinet, drawer, and book
For anything alive that they can prey on

A feisty fer-de-lance
Slithers through your pants

Then falls asleep inside your mother's purse

A speckled anaconda
Steals the family Honda
And races down the driveway in reverse

A skink inserts her snoutlet
In an open kitchen outlet
Her body starts to phosphoresce with light

There's a momentary riot
As all the others try it
Soon all the snakes, like neon tubes, ignite

Serpents madly wrangling
Upside-down, dangling
Bungee-jumping off your house's gutter

Cowering in boxes
Tangled up in sockses
Buried to their necks in peanut butter

Snakes as drapes
As measuring tapes
As animated cleaners for your ears

Snakes as garden hoses
For trimming hairy noses

Snakes as rubber bands and spears

Snakes as playground swings
Snakes as teething rings
As thermometers and nifty stethoscopes

Snakes as clarinets

Snakes as bayonets

For tug-of-wars, snakes as giant ropes

There've been no snake attacks
So you've started to relax
Up above the mayhem, in your lair

When your skin breaks out in bumps
Your respiration jumps
And something deep within you says beware

You open up the shutter
Your heartbeat starts to flutter
For the one and only thing that
   you can spy

Resolutely staring at you
Absolutely glaring at you
Larger than a tabletop: an eye!

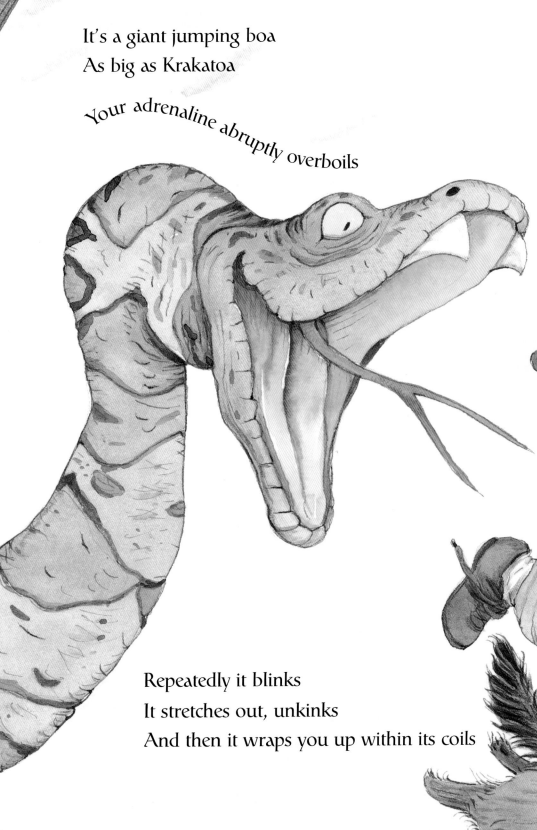

It's a giant jumping boa
As big as Krakatoa

Your adrenaline abruptly overboils

Repeatedly it blinks
It stretches out, unkinks
And then it wraps you up within its coils

You feel a faint restriction
Of serpentine constriction
In moments you can barely breathe or cough

You face a scary issue
Is the boa going to squish you?

It's impossible to yank the serpent off

Even though you're bony
He clings like macaroni

It feels like you're about to be deceased

Then he hisses in your ear,
"I truly like you, dear,

And sssssssomeday (maybe) you will be releasssssssed."